THE GREAT BIBLE DISCOVERY

THE CHURCH AT THE END OF THE FIRST CENTURY

THE BIBLE IS A BEST-SELLER. IT IS ALSO ONE OF THE MASTER-WORKS OF WORLD LITERATURE - SO IMPORTANT THAT UNIVERSITIES TODAY TEACH 'NON-RELIGIOUS' BIBLE COURSES TO HELP STUDENTS WHO CHOOSE TO STUDY WESTERN LITERATURE.

THE BIBLE POSSESSES AN AMAZING POWER TO FASCINATE YOUNG AND OLD ALIKE.

ONE REASON FOR THIS UNIVERSAL APPEAL IS THAT IT DEALS WITH BASIC HUMAN LONGINGS, EMOTIONS, RELATIONSHIPS. 'ALL THE WORLD IS HERE.' ANOTHER REASON IS THAT SO MUCH OF THE BIBLE CONSISTS OF STORIES. THEY ARE FULL OF MEANING BUT EASY TO REMEMBER.

HERE ARE THOSE STORIES, PRESENTED SIMPLY AND WITH A MINIMUM OF EXPLANATION. WE HAVE LEFT THE TEXT TO SPEAK FOR ITSELF. GIFTED ARTISTS USE THE ACTION-STRIP TECHNIQUE TO BRING THE BIBLE'S DEEP MESSAGE TO READERS OF ALL AGES. THEIR DRAWINGS ARE BASED ON INFORMATION FROM ARCHAEOLOGICAL DISCOVERIES COVERING FIFTEEN CENTURIES.

AN ANCIENT BOOK - PRESENTED FOR THE PEOPLE OF THE SECOND MILLENNIUM. A RELIGIOUS BOOK - PRESENTED FREE FROM THE INTERPRETATION OF ANY PARTICULAR CHURCH. A UNIVERSAL BOOK - PRESENTED IN A FORM THAT ALL MAY ENJOY.

OM publishing
CARLISLE, UK

24

The Book of Acts shows how Christianity spread from Jerusalem westward into the Greek and Roman world. But among those who listened to Peter on the Day of Pentecost there had been pilgrims from Africa and from eastern countries - 'Parthians, Medes and Elamites; residents of Mesopotamia, Egypt . . .' By the end of the first century there were churches in these countries. Christianity did not originate in 'the west'. It was destined to become a world-wide faith.

Most of the first Christians lived in cities. They came from the lower and middle working classes - slaves, freedmen, tradesmen. The church was not yet a centralized organization but the Holy Spirit guided its leaders as they relied upon the apostles' teaching in the gospels and the letters Paul and other apostolic men had written.

These Christians faced many difficulties. Their neighbours suspected them because they were 'different'. Because their homes contained no images of the gods they were accused of being atheists. They were said to sacrifice children and commit incest when they met for the eucharistic meal. Thus they were an obvious target for accusations of having started the fire which destroyed Rome in AD 64 , when Nero was emperor.

When the Jews of Palestine rebelled against Rome Jewish Christians, whom the Romans had previously classified as followers of the Jewish faith, which was officially tolerated, began to separate themselves from their fellow Jews. In the long run this meant that they were guilty of following an 'unauthorized religion'. They were not always proceeded against but were always in danger of being accused.

In addition, it became increasingly common for Roman emperors to demand that their subjects should publicly burn incense on an altar to the God Caesar as a sign of loyalty. The Emperor Domitian enforced this in AD 81. Many Christians refused to obey and were consequently condemned to death in the arena.

It is against this background that we should read the Book of Revelation, containing the visions of 'John' on the island of Patmos. Tradition identifies him as the Apostle John who wrote the Fourth Gospel.

ACTS 21-38
COLOSSIANS 3
EPHESIANS 4
REVELATION

THE CHURCH AT THE END OF THE FIRST CENTURY

First published as *Découvrir la Bible* 1983

First edition © Larousse S.A. 1984
24-volume series adaptation by Mike Jacklin © Knowledge Unlimited 1994
This edition © OM Publishing 1995

01 00 99 98 97 96 95   7 6 5 4 3 2 1

OM Publishing is an imprint of Send the Light Ltd.,
P.O. Box 300, Carlisle, Cumbria CA3 0QS, U.K.

Introductions: Peter Cousins

British Library Cataloguing in Publication Data
A catalogue record for this book is available from the British Library
ISBN 1-85078-228-8

Printed in Singapore by Tien Wah Press (Pte) Ltd.

PAUL

from Jerusalem to Rome

I HOPE YOU'LL BE STAYING WITH US FOR SOME TIME, PAUL.

FOR A FEW DAYS, PHILIP... THE FEAST OF PENTECOST IS COMING, AND I'M STILL NOT IN JERUSALEM!

SCENARIO: Etienne DAHLER
DRAWING: Victor de LA FUENTE

AT THE END OF HIS THIRD VOYAGE, ON HIS WAY TO JERUSALEM, PAUL STOPPED AT CAESAREA. HE STAYED IN THE HOME OF PHILIP, ONE OF THE SEVEN DEACONS IN THE FIRST CHRISTIAN COMMUNITY.

PAUL! AGABUS IS HERE. HE HAS COME FROM JUDAEA TO SPEAK TO YOU.

AGABUS, THE PROPHET... WE MUST LISTEN TO HIM, LUKE.

PAUL, DON'T GO TO JERUSALEM!

YOU SEE WHAT'S WAITING FOR YOU!

SO? I'M READY, NOT ONLY TO BE TIED UP IN JERUSALEM, BUT EVEN TO DIE FOR THE SAKE OF THE LORD JESUS.

AGABUS CAME FORWARD, AND ASKED PAUL FOR HIS BELT. THEN...

THE HOLY SPIRIT SAYS: THE OWNER OF THIS BELT WILL BE TIED UP LIKE THIS BY THE JEWS IN JERUSALEM, AND THEY'LL HAND HIM OVER TO THE PAGANS!

AND A FEW DAYS LATER PAUL TOOK THE ROAD TO THE HOLY CITY.

3

THE DAY AFTER HE HAD ARRIVED IN JERUSALEM, PAUL WENT TO SEE JAMES AND THE LEADERS OF THE CHURCH.

GOD BE PRAISED FOR BRINGING YOU BACK TO US, PAUL!

BROTHERS, IT'S A JOY FOR US ALL TO BE WITH YOU AGAIN!

AND PAUL GAVE THEM A FULL ACCOUNT OF EVERYTHING THAT HAD HAPPENED TO HIM AMONG THE PAGANS. THEN JAMES SPOKE...

PAUL, I MUST TELL YOU THAT THERE'S A RUMOUR THAT YOU'RE ENCOURAGING THE JEWS TO TURN AWAY FROM THE LAW OF MOSES.

THAT'S NOT TRUE! ALL I SAY IS THAT THE PAGANS DON'T NEED TO BE CIRCUMCISED. I'M JUST CARRYING OUT WHAT WE DECIDED HERE ALMOST 10 YEARS AGO.

YOU MUST SHOW EVERYONE THAT YOU ALSO KEEP THE LAW... FOUR OF US HAVE MADE A VOW...

YOU'RE NOT THE ONLY ONES!

I WAS INTENDING TO GO TO THE TEMPLE TOMORROW FOR THE SEVEN DAYS OF CLEANSING. I'LL GO WITH YOU.

PAUL, FORGIVE ME...

THE NEXT DAY...

4

KILL HIM!

DEATH!

HE'S AN ENEMY OF THE EMPIRE!

MAY I SPEAK TO YOU?

YOU SPEAK GREEK? THEN YOU'RE NOT THAT EGYPTIAN WHO STARTED A REVOLUTION?

NO, I'M A JEW, BORN IN TARSUS IN CILICIA... WILL YOU LET ME SPEAK TO THE PEOPLE?

YES, PAUL; YOU MAY DO THAT.

SO PAUL SPOKE TO THE CROWD IN HEBREW. HE TOLD THEM ABOUT HIS EARLY LIFE, THEN HOW HE BECAME A CHRISTIAN...

THE LORD SAID TO ME: 'GO! I WILL SEND YOU FAR AWAY, TO THE PAGANS...'

THAT'S ENOUGH! HE'S NOT FIT TO LIVE!

...AND THE MOB BECAME EVEN MORE DANGEROUS...

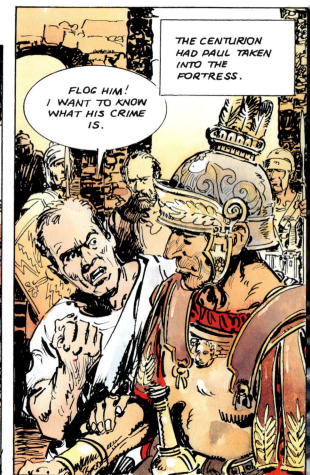

THE CENTURION HAD PAUL TAKEN INTO THE FORTRESS.

FLOG HIM! I WANT TO KNOW WHAT HIS CRIME IS.

PAUL KNEW VERY WELL THAT IN THE SANHEDRIN THE PHARISEES DISAGREED WITH THE SADDUCEES, SO HE WAS CLEVER IN THE WAY HE BEGAN HIS SPEECH.

BROTHERS, I'M A PHARISEE, THE SON OF A PHARISEE. AND I'M BEING JUDGED BECAUSE WE HOPE THAT THE DEAD WILL RISE AGAIN!

YOU HAVE TO BE A PHARISEE TO BELIEVE THAT NONSENSE!

WHAT A JOKE!

BE QUIET, YOU SADDUCEES! THIS MAN IS RIGHT!

THEY SHOUTED LOUDER, AND CAME TO BLOWS... THEN THE TRIBUNE...

BRING THE PRISONER TO ME BEFORE THEY TEAR HIM TO PIECES!

THE NEXT NIGHT THE LORD APPEARED TO PAUL.

BE BRAVE! YOU'VE WITNESSED FOR ME HERE IN JERUSALEM, AND YOU MUST DO SO IN ROME AS WELL.

MEANWHILE, ABOUT 40 JEWS MET...

WE SWEAR NOT TO EAT OR DRINK UNTIL PAUL HAS BEEN KILLED!

THE CONSPIRATORS CAME TO AN AGREEMENT WITH THE CHIEF PRIESTS.

RIGHT! TOMORROW I'LL ASK THE TRIBUNE TO LET US QUESTION PAUL AGAIN...

...AND WE'LL MAKE SURE HE NEVER APPEARS BEFORE THE SANHEDRIN!

BUT SEVERAL PHARISEES GOT TO HEAR OF THE PLOT. ONE OF THEM WAS PAUL'S BROTHER-IN-LAW...

SON, RUN TO THE FORTRESS, AND WARN YOUR UNCLE!

RIGHT AWAY, FATHER!

PAUL SENT THE LAD TO THE TRIBUNE.

NOW YOU KNOW IT ALL, SIR... YOU MUST PROTECT MY UNCLE!

I'LL TAKE GOOD CARE OF HIM, SON. DON'T YOU WORRY!

I'M IN LUCK! NOW I CAN GET RID OF THIS DIFFICULT CASE...

FIVE DAYS LATER THE HIGH PRIEST ANANIAS, SEVERAL ELDERS, AND TERTULLUS, A LAWYER, CAME FROM JERUSALEM AND APPEARED BEFORE FELIX.

LET THE ACCUSERS BEGIN! I'M LISTENING, TERTULLUS!

MOST EXCELLENT FELIX, I SHALL BE BRIEF. THIS MAN IS A PEST! HE STARTS RIOTS AMONG THE JEWS ALL OVER THE WORLD. HE'S ONE OF THE LEADERS OF THE NAZARENE SECT...

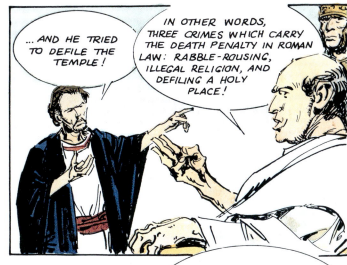

...AND HE TRIED TO DEFILE THE TEMPLE!

IN OTHER WORDS, THREE CRIMES WHICH CARRY THE DEATH PENALTY IN ROMAN LAW: RABBLE-ROUSING, ILLEGAL RELIGION, AND DEFILING A HOLY PLACE!

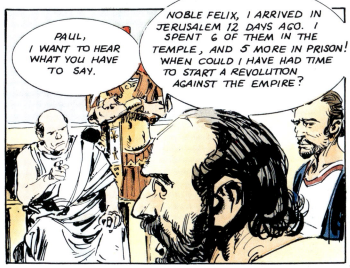

PAUL, I WANT TO HEAR WHAT YOU HAVE TO SAY.

NOBLE FELIX, I ARRIVED IN JERUSALEM 12 DAYS AGO. I SPENT 6 OF THEM IN THE TEMPLE, AND 5 MORE IN PRISON! WHEN COULD I HAVE HAD TIME TO START A REVOLUTION AGAINST THE EMPIRE?

AND I SWEAR TO YOU: I WORSHIP THE GOD OF MY FATHERS. I BELIEVE THE LAW AND THE PROPHETS. LIKE MY BROTHERS, THE PHARISEES, I BELIEVE THAT THE DEAD WILL RISE AGAIN...

...FINALLY, I WENT TO THE TEMPLE TO FAST AND PRAY. IT WAS THEY WHO STARTED THE RIOT, NOT I!

THIS IS A DIFFICULT CASE. I SHALL RESERVE JUDGEMENT UNTIL THERE HAS BEEN A COMPLETE INQUIRY.

...CLOSELY FOLLOWED BY THE LEADING MEN OF JERUSALEM...

VERY SOON, IN THE COURTROOM IN CAESAREA, NEW CHARGES WERE BROUGHT AGAINST PAUL, BUT WITHOUT ANY PROOF...

I REFUSE! I WOULDN'T BE JUDGED THERE; I WOULD BE KILLED!

LIAR!

HOW DARE YOU?

I'VE ALREADY SAID, AND I SAY IT AGAIN FOR THE LAST TIME: I'VE DONE NOTHING WRONG AGAINST THE LAW, AGAINST THE TEMPLE, OR AGAINST THE EMPEROR!

PAUL, I'M NOT ABLE TO DEAL WITH YOUR CASE. DON'T YOU WANT TO BE TRIED BY YOUR OWN PEOPLE IN JERUSALEM?

IF THIS COURT SAYS IT CAN'T DEAL WITH MY CASE, THEN... I APPEAL TO THE EMPEROR!

THE ROOM WAS DEADLY QUIET. FESTUS WAS UPSET, AND WENT OUT TO CONSULT HIS ADVISERS...

THEN...

YOU'VE APPEALED TO THE EMPEROR, SO YOU'LL GO TO THE EMPEROR!

A FEW DAYS LATER KING AGRIPPA II, GRANDSON OF HEROD THE GREAT, WHO NOW RULED OVER A SMALL REGION TO THE NORTH-EAST OF PALESTINE, CAME WITH HIS SISTER BERNICE, TO WELCOME THE NEW GOVERNOR.

I WOULD VERY MUCH LIKE TO HEAR THIS FELLOW...

NO TROUBLE! I'VE ARRANGED A SPECIAL HEARING FOR TOMORROW...

EVER SINCE I GOT HERE, I'VE HAD TO DEAL WITH A PETTY AFFAIR THAT YOU WOULD BE INTER-ESTED TO HEAR ABOUT, AGRIPPA.

PLEASE, FESTUS, DON'T KEEP ME ON TENTERHOOKS ANY LONGER!

GUARDS! BRING IN THE EMPEROR'S PRISONER!

NEXT DAY...

KING AGRIPPA, AND ALL HERE WITH US, THIS IS THE MAN WHO'LL SOON BE LEAVING FOR ROME. I WANT YOUR ADVICE BEFORE WRITING TO THE EMPEROR ABOUT HIM.

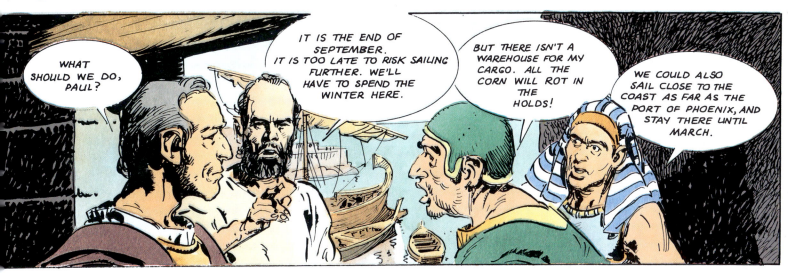

IN ROME PETER ENRICHED THE CHRISTIANS THROUGH HIS FIRST-HAND INFORMATION ABOUT THE LIFE OF JESUS. MARK DEPENDED ON IT IN WRITING HIS GOSPEL.

PAUL'S CASE CAME UP, AND HE WAS SET FREE IN AD 63. ONCE MORE HE BEGAN TO TRAVEL IN THE EAST: EPHESUS, CRETE, MACEDONIA, NICOPOLIS...

IN JULY 64, ROME WAS ALMOST DESTROYED BY FIRE. NERO BLAMED THE CHRISTIANS FOR IT. A TERRIBLE PERSECUTION BROKE OUT.

A PERSON COULD BE TORTURED JUST FOR BEING A CHRISTIAN, AND PAUL WAS ARRESTED AGAIN.

HE WAS TAKEN BACK TO ROME, SHUT AWAY IN THE MAMERTINE PRISON, AND MOST OF THE CHRISTIANS KEPT AWAY FROM HIM.

PETER WAS ARRESTED ALSO. HE WOULD SOON BE CRUCIFIED IN NERO'S CIRCUS.

BECAUSE HE WAS A ROMAN CITIZEN, PAUL WAS BEHEADED. AFTER THEY HAD LIVED AND DIED TO SERVE THE CHURCH, THE PRINCE OF THE APOSTLES AND THE APOSTLE TO THE PAGANS WERE UNITED ONCE MORE.

IN THE SPRING OF AD 70 THE NEW EMPEROR, VESPASIAN, HURLED 60 000 MEN OF HIS LEGIONS AGAINST JERUSALEM, TO CRUSH THE JEWISH REBELLION WHICH HAD LASTED FOR FOUR YEARS.

AT THEIR HEAD WAS HIS OWN SON, TITUS.

THE VISIONS OF JOHN
THE BOOK OF REVELATION

THE TERRIBLE NEWS SPREAD THROUGH THE HOLY CITY, FULL OF PILGRIMS COME TO CELEBRATE PASSOVER.

THE ROMANS ARE COMING! BOLT YOUR DOORS!

SCENARIO: Etienne DAHLER
DRAWING: Raymond POÏVET

26

THE NEWS SOON REACHED EPHESUS IN ASIA MINOR, WHERE THE APOSTLE JOHN HAD BEEN LIVING FOR SOME YEARS.

JOHN, HOW COULD GOD LET SUCH A THING HAPPEN?

THE MASTER FORETOLD IT! HE SAID: 'NOT ONE STONE OF THIS BUILDING WILL BE LEFT IN ITS PLACE.'

HE ALSO SAID: 'THAT WILL BE ONLY THE BEGINNING OF THE TROUBLES. YOU'LL BE PERSECUTED FOR MY SAKE.'

BUT...

I REMEMBER SOMETHING ELSE JESUS SAID: 'WHEN THE GOOD NEWS OF THE KINGDOM HAS REACHED TO THE ENDS OF THE EARTH, THE END WILL COME.'

JOHN, WE'VE BEEN WAITING FOR YOU. MANY OF THE BROTHERS ARE VERY UPSET BY THE NEWS THAT JERUSALEM HAS FALLEN.

I'LL SPEAK TO THEM.

30

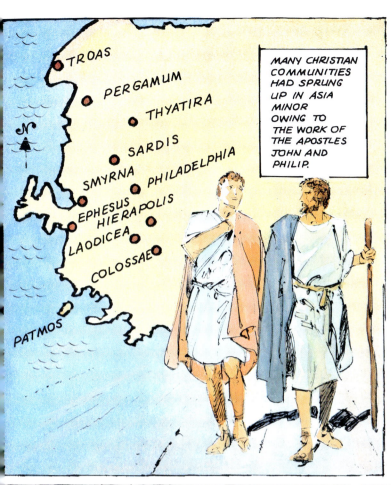

MANY CHRISTIAN COMMUNITIES HAD SPRUNG UP IN ASIA MINOR OWING TO THE WORK OF THE APOSTLES JOHN AND PHILIP.

TWO MESSENGERS SOON ARRIVED IN HIERAPOLIS.

LET'S GO AND SEE PHILIP FIRST.

JOHN THINKS WE OUGHT TO BE DOING MORE PREACHING.

HE'S AFRAID THAT SOON WE WON'T BE ABLE TO ACT FREELY.

TELL JOHN THAT HERE WE'RE READY TO GIVE OUR LIVES FOR THE LORD.

I'LL SEND A BROTHER TO EPHESUS. MORE THAN EVER BEFORE, WE MUST STAND TOGETHER!

GOD BE WITH YOU!

31

34

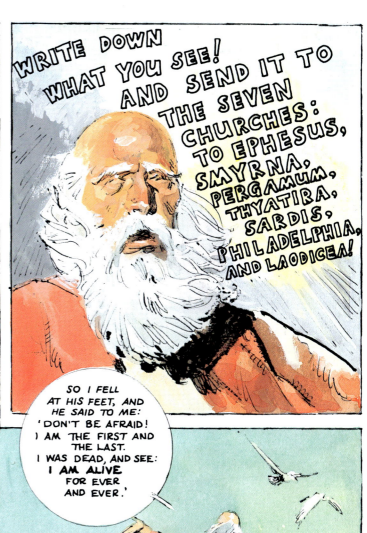

A GREAT SIGN APPEARED IN THE SKY: A WOMAN WHOSE DRESS WAS THE SUN, WHO HAD THE MOON UNDER HER FEET, AND A CROWN OF TWELVE STARS ON HER HEAD...

A SECOND SIGN APPEARED, A HUGE DRAGON. IT GOT READY TO DEVOUR THE CHILD AS SOON AS IT WAS BORN.

SHE WAS ABOUT TO GIVE BIRTH TO A CHILD...

THE BOY WAS SNATCHED AWAY AND TAKEN TO GOD, WHILE THE WOMAN FLED... THEN THE DRAGON HAD TO FIGHT THE HEAVENLY ARMY...

...IT WAS THROWN DOWN TO THE EARTH. THEN IT ATTACKED THE WOMAN'S OTHER CHILDREN, THOSE WHO KEEP GOD'S COMMANDMENTS...

THE WOMAN GAVE BIRTH TO A BOY.

...AND ARE FAITHFUL TO JESUS.

44

THEN ANOTHER BEAST CAME UP OUT OF THE SEA, AND THE DRAGON GAVE IT HIS OWN STRENGTH AND GREAT POWER.

SOON THE BEAST RULED OVER ALL TRIBES, PEOPLES, LANGUAGES AND NATIONS.

THEN ANOTHER BEAST CAME UP OUT OF THE EARTH. IT LOOKED LIKE THE LAMB, BUT IT SPOKE LIKE THE DRAGON.

IT DECEIVED THE PEOPLE ON THE EARTH, AND MADE THEM WORSHIP THE FIRST BEAST.

IT PUT A MARK ON EVERYBODY, SMALL AND GREAT, RICH AND POOR...

...AND NO ONE COULD BUY OR SELL UNLESS HE WAS MARKED WITH THE NUMBER OF THE BEAST, 666.

THEN AN ANGEL CALLED TO ME...

COME! I'LL SHOW YOU THE JUDGEMENT OF THE GREAT PROSTITUTE WHO LIVES ON THE EDGE OF THE OCEANS.

BABYLON

ALL WHO'VE HAD DEALINGS WITH HER WILL FIGHT AGAINST THE LAMB, BUT HE'LL DEFEAT THEM, BECAUSE HE'S THE LORD OF LORDS.

IN THE END THE BEAST ITSELF TURNED AGAINST THE PROSTITUTE.

SHE HAS FALLEN! BABYLON THE GREAT HAS FALLEN!

HOW AWFUL! BABYLON, ONE HOUR WAS ENOUGH TO JUDGE YOU!

48